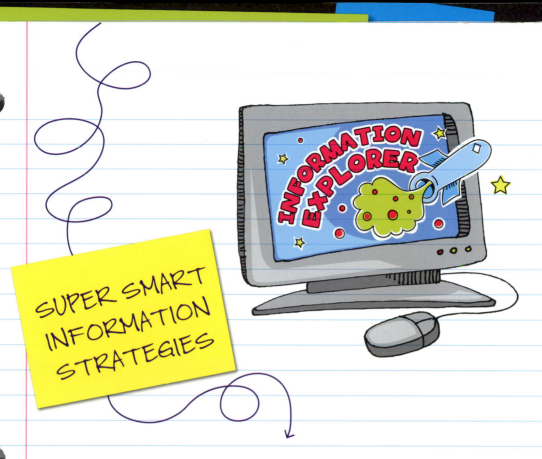

SUPER SMART INFORMATION STRATEGIES

FIRE AWAY:

ASKING GREAT INTERVIEW QUESTIONS

by Ann Truesdell

CHERRY LAKE PUBLISHING • ANN ARBOR, MICHIGAN

CHERRY LAKE Publishing

Published in the United States of America
by Cherry Lake Publishing
Ann Arbor, Michigan
www.cherrylakepublishing.com

Content Adviser: Gail Dickinson, PhD,
Associate Professor, Old Dominion University,
Norfolk, Virginia

Photo Credits: Cover, ©Lisa F. Young/Dreamstime.com; page 4, ©Adam Gregor/ Shutterstock, Inc.; page 5, ©Faraways/Shutterstock, Inc.; page 8, ©Blend Images/Shutterstock, Inc.; page 9, ©Steve Bower/Shutterstock, Inc.; page 10, ©KobchaiMa/Shutterstock, Inc.; page 11, ©Christopher Meder - Photography/ Shutterstock, Inc.; page 12, ©Yuri Arcurs/Shutterstock, Inc.; page 13, ©Darrin Henry/Shutterstock, Inc.; pages 14 and 17, ©Showface/Dreamstime.com; page 18, ©Elena Elisseeva/Dreamstime.com; page 19, ©Canettistock/Dreamstime. com; page 20, ©Dmitriy Shironosov/Shutterstock, Inc.; page 21, ©iStockphoto. com/Yobro10; page 22, ©iStockphoto.com/lisafx; page 24, ©Rtimages/ Shutterstock, Inc.; page 25, ©Xalanx/Dreamstime.com; page 26, ©Jacek Chabraszewski/Dreamstime.com; page 27, ©Ron Chapple/Dreamstime.com; page 28, ©Jonathan Ross/Dreamstime.com

Library of Congress Cataloging-in-Publication Data
Truesdell, Ann.
    Fire away : asking great interview questions / by Ann Truesdell.
        pages cm. — (Information explorer)
    Includes bibliographical references and index.
    ISBN 978-1-61080-481-3 (lib. bdg.) — ISBN 978-1-61080-655-8 (pbk.) — ISBN 978-1-61080-568-1 (e-book)
    1. Interviewing —Juvenile literature. 2. Research—Methodology—Juvenile literature. I. Title.
    BF637.I4T785 2013   2012003085
    158.3'9—dc23

Cherry Lake Publishing would like to acknowledge
the work of The Partnership for 21st Century Skills.
Please visit *www.21stcenturyskills.org* for more information.

Printed in the United States of America
Corporate Graphics Inc.
July 2012
CLFA11

A NOTE TO PARENTS AND TEACHERS: Please remind your children how to stay safe online before they do the activities in this book.

A NOTE TO KIDS: Always remember your safety comes first!

Table of Contents

CHAPTER ONE
Why Do an Interview?

Job interviews help employers find the right people to work at their companies.

"How did you feel when it happened?"

"What was your favorite part?"

"What are some things you learned?"

"Why did you decide to do that?"

These are some of the many questions that people might ask during an **interview**. An interview is all about asking people questions. It can be a one-on-one interview, where one person asks another some questions. It can also be a small group question-and-answer session.

People interview each other for many different reasons. You've probably seen interviews on television before. News shows interview people to learn more about an event that happened. Talk shows interview people to find out more about the people themselves. You may have seen your favorite athletes interviewed on TV after a game. There are also job interviews, where companies interview people who have applied for a job. The companies ask questions to find out more about the people and decide who should get the job.

Interviewing can also be an important research tool for students. Good researchers don't rely only on print and Internet sources. They consider all of the sources

Have you ever seen someone being interviewed on a TV news show?

available to them. Sources can often include living people and their stories. People often have important information you can't get from other sources. You might interview someone to find out more about a historical event. You could ask someone questions about his or her career, especially if it is a career you are interested in for yourself. It is also a great idea to interview someone who is an expert on a topic that you are researching. For example, if you are researching elephants, you could interview a zookeeper who cares for them. Interviews can be helpful resources when the topic you have chosen doesn't have many books or articles about it yet. Interviews give you an insider's look at the subject you are researching!

Interviews are different from surveys. Surveys are lists of short, simple questions given to many people at once. Interviews let you speak with someone face-to-face, and you can ask many different questions. As the interviewee answers your questions, you might discover new things to ask about. The interview could go in a different direction from how you originally planned it!

TRY THIS!

An interview is helpful for many different types of research. Sometimes, the most difficult part of interviewing is finding the right interviewee. Brainstorm whom you might interview to gather information about the following topics.

Some interviewees might be people you already know. Others might be experts you have never met.

TEACHER

MAYOR

SINGER

Whom could you interview about:
- the life cycle of an insect?
- what it is like to work in a school?
- voting laws in your hometown?
- which foods are most nutritious?
- how computers work?
- what it is like to act or play music in front of a crowd?
- what schools are like in Germany?

To get a copy of this activity, visit www.cherrylakepublishing.com/activities.

7

CHAPTER TWO
Preparing to Interview

An airplane pilot would be an excellent source of information if you wanted to learn more about how flight works.

A good interview requires a lot of preparation. The preparation will probably take much longer than the actual interview! It's tempting to rush into an interview. But your results will be better if you are well prepared.

First, you must learn enough about your topic to help you choose a good interviewee. You will have to gather **background information** about your topic.

Background information is the research that you conduct before getting too involved in the project. It helps you decide what resources you will need to do your main research. It will also help you determine if your interviewee is a good resource for your topic. Let's say you want to learn about flight. A pilot would be a good interviewee if you want to know about airplanes. But you might want to learn about other kinds of flight. You could interview someone who works with hot air balloons, kites, or even birds!

A hot air balloon operator might be an even more interesting interviewee than an airplane pilot.

Many interviews can be conducted over the phone.

Next, you must find a way to contact the person you wish to interview. Ask your parents or teachers for help with this step. You should never contact or meet with strangers on your own.

Be very polite and professional when you ask someone for an interview. Explain why you want to interview him or her, and what information you hope to gather. Once the person agrees to the interview, you need to decide how, where, and when it will take place. Interviewing in person is usually best, but it is not always possible. Other options include using video chat on your computer or doing the interview by phone. Plan to do the interview in a quiet and calm place, with a parent or teacher nearby. Determine when the interview will happen. Make sure you allow some time to prepare for the interview. You will need at least a few days to gather more research and form your questions. Finally, ask your interviewee if he or she is comfortable with the interview being recorded.

Once you have scheduled your interview, it is time to do more research on your topic. It is very important not to skip this step. You need this information so you'll understand what the interviewee is telling you. It will be hard to tell the difference between opinions and facts. Plus, you don't want to spend too much time talking

If your interviewee is too busy to meet in person, you might still be able to conduct the interview using e-mail, video chat, or an instant messaging program.

about the basic parts of your topic. Your research will also help you come up with good questions to ask during your interview. After your research is done, make a list of things you want to learn from the interviewee.

The best interview questions are ones that get your interviewee talking. Do not ask too many questions that will lead to a short answer such as "yes" or "no." Those are called closed-ended questions. You want questions that make your interviewee tell you a story or give you details. These are called open-ended questions.

Older people might be able to tell you interesting stories about historic events.

Write down plenty of good questions so you don't run out of things to ask during the interview.

Open-ended questions often make your interviewee give opinions in addition to facts. "How old were you during the Vietnam War?" is a closed-ended question. It will probably result in an answer like "I was 11 years old." An open-ended question would be "What do you remember about the Vietnam War?" It invites your interviewee to open up about his or her own experiences.

Make a list of at least 15 good questions to take to your interview. Have these questions written down or typed out in a way that allows space for you to take notes. This is helpful even if you are planning to record your interview. Keep in mind that you might not need all of the questions on your list. Interviews sometimes take their own course, but it's always best to be prepared.

Using a video camera makes it easier to review your interview after it is over.

Finally, decide on how you will **document** the interview. Writing down notes during the interview is always a good idea. However, it is difficult to write down everything that happens. Find out if your interviewee will allow you to record the interview. Some interviewees might prefer that you only record the sound of the interview. Others might feel fine about letting you record video. Always respect your interviewee. He or she is doing you a favor by allowing the interview.

You will need some equipment to record your interview. If a video is allowed, then you will need a video camera or another device that can record long videos. This might be a computer with a built-in camera, a phone, or an iPod. Are you are using FaceTime or Skype to interview? If so, you can use screen capture software on your computer to record it. This will record the video and sound that you see and hear on your computer.

If you want to record only the sound of the interview, you can use a handheld digital recorder or the voice recorder software on an iPod, a phone, or a computer. Be sure to test your equipment long before you do your interview. Test it again on the day of the interview. It's also a good idea to have at least one backup method in case something goes wrong.

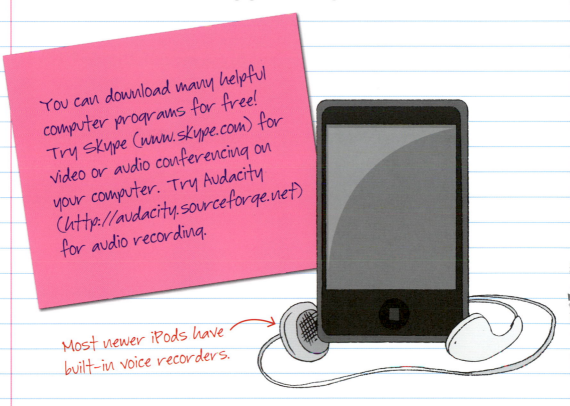

You can download many helpful computer programs for free! Try Skype (www.skype.com) for video or audio conferencing on your computer. Try Audacity (http://audacity.sourceforge.net) for audio recording.

Most newer iPods have built-in voice recorders.

TRY THIS!

Asking the right questions can be tough, but it gets easier with practice. Pair up with another student in your class. Find out which activities he or she participates in after school. Using the rules below as your guide, write down 10 questions to ask your classmate about the activity. You might have to look up some background on the activity first.

To get a copy of this activity, visit www.cherrylakepublishing.com/activities.

INTERVIEW QUESTION RULES:

1. No more than two closed-ended questions. For example:
   How long have you been taking gymnastics classes?

2. Start by asking a few fact-based questions about the activity. For example:
   Can you describe what happens at an average gymnastics competition?

3. Next, ask questions that get your classmate to give opinions about the activity. For example:
   What do you like most about gymnastics?

What questions did you come up with? How did they compare to the questions above?

CHAPTER THREE
The Interview

Use your best manners when you meet your interviewee.

The day of the interview has arrived! Remember to bring your list of questions, a notebook, a pencil, and your recording equipment. When you meet your interviewee, greet him or her with a smile and a polite hello. If you are meeting in person, offer a firm handshake. Introduce yourself if this is your first time meeting face-to-face. No matter what, be sure to thank the person for agreeing to the interview. Be as polite as possible throughout the interview. Remember that this person is taking time to help you.

You can conduct an interview anywhere there is space for two people to talk.

If you are recording the interview, set up your recording equipment and give it a quick test. If you have any extra time before the interview begins, take a few notes about your surroundings. Write down what your interviewee looks like and is wearing. Are you at the interviewee's home or workplace? You might take notes about pictures that hang on walls or decorations that you notice. Things like these are little clues about who your interviewee is. You might ask the interviewee questions about pictures or decorations that interest you.

Time to ask some questions! Do not give your interviewee your list of questions to read through and answer. That would result in a boring interview. The best **interviewers** start out with one or two closed-ended questions. These can help break the ice and put you both at ease. Then, start asking some open-ended questions. Remember that an interview never goes exactly as planned. The questions that you wrote down are really just a general guide. Many good interviews start to sound like a conversation between two people, rather than a formal question-and-answer session.

Be an active listener. Active listening is when you listen very carefully to what someone is saying and think about the answers you're hearing. Try hard to

Pay careful attention to the interviewee's responses.

understand what it is the person is speaking about.
Look at the person's facial expressions and body move-
ments. The things you notice will help you understand
what the interviewee is saying and how he or she feels
about the topic.

If you are actively listening, the next question
you ask might not be the next one on your list. It
might even be a question that you did not think to
write down. You may need to ask your interviewee to
elaborate on an answer. You may also ask questions
to make sure you understood the interviewee correctly.

Don't be afraid to refer back to your
list of questions during the interview.

Your notes do not need to be as detailed if you are recording the interview.

For example, you might ask, "Do you mean...?" and then use your own words to say what the person just said. If you are interviewing for a research project, you need to know your information well. Going over the interviewee's responses with him or her can help you understand the topic better. It also gives the interviewee a chance to add more information or correct any errors.

Take some notes during the interview to help you make sense of your thoughts and your interviewee's answers. If you are not recording the interview, you will need to take very complete notes. It is impossible to write down every word that is said, so your notes should simply be a **summary** of your interviewee's

Always remember to thank your interviewee for his or her time.

answers. You can also include any thoughts that come to mind during the interview. Jot down words you don't know or questions that you think of while your interviewee is speaking. Then ask him or her to explain them before going to the next question. You can also take notes on how the interviewee moves and behaves. Does he or she get excited about certain questions? Comment on any emotions that you sense.

When you are finished with your questions, or when time is up, the interview is complete. Thank your interviewee again. Ask if you can contact him or her with any other questions that you think of later. You are sure to think of another question as you move on to the final steps of the interview process!

TRY THIS!

Pair up with your partner from the last activity to practice interviewing each other. Bring your questions and some paper and a pencil to take notes. You might also want to record the interview!

After the interview, discuss how it went with your partner. Did you stick to your questions, or did you let a natural conversation take place? What did you learn? Did any of your partner's answers surprise you? Take another look at your notes. Was taking notes easy for you? Is it easy to read your notes now that you are finished with the interview? How could you have improved the interview?

23

To get a copy of this activity, visit www.cherrylakepublishing.com/activities.

CHAPTER FOUR
After the Interview

If you recorded the interview, watch or listen to your recording and take notes on anything you missed the first time.

A good interviewer isn't finished when the interview ends. There is still much to do. If possible, you should write down your thoughts about the interview as soon as it is over. Look back at your notes and fill in any gaps that you see. Maybe you wrote down some **abbreviations**. Now is the time to go back and turn them into full words. Make sense of any words that are hard to read. If you were writing very fast, some of your words might look like scribbles. Some notes might not make any sense if you cannot remember which question you asked. Figure this out while it is fresh in your memory. The sooner after the interview that you do all this, the better! It is hard to remember exactly what you were thinking even just a few days after the interview.

You will also want to make some additional notes that you may not have made during the interview. Think about how you felt during the interview and

Reviewing your notes will help prepare you for the final part of your project.

You may need to do some extra research to help you understand all of your interviewee's answers.

how your interviewee might have felt. Did the interviewee seem happy to be interviewed, or nervous? Did he or she offer any additional information that you didn't think to ask about? Were all of your questions answered?

In the days following the interview, you should conduct any additional research that will help you with your project. Your interviewee may have given you some ideas of what else you still need to research. You might check some other sources to see what they say about your topic. You need many different sources to help form your project. This will help you understand which answers from your interview were facts and which were either opinions or **biased**. Bias can happen when people give their side of a story without including anyone else's.

Revisit the interview before you start writing or preparing your final report. Reread your questions, notes, and anything you wrote down right after the interview

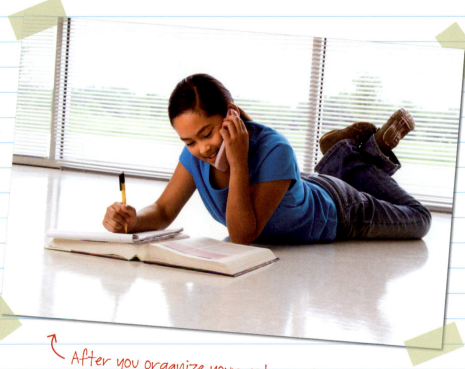

After you organize your notes and do additional research, you might need to contact your interviewee and ask a few more questions.

ended. If you recorded your interview, watch or listen to the recording. Take more notes if you need to. Try slowing down parts or listening to them a couple of times. This will help you get direct **quotations** to use in your project. Be extra careful to write down exactly what your interviewee said word by word. You might even note how your interviewee said it. For example, did he or she seem happy, sad, or excited? If you have a video recording, you can note any facial expressions or hand motions the interviewee made.

Always write down your interviewee's exact words when using a direct quotation.

TRY THIS!

Look over your interview notes from the last activity. Review the notes and consider if there was any bias. What information from your partner is probably true? Double-check this with another resource. What information is opinion? Why might your classmate feel a certain way about the activity?

You should also consider that some information might be true for only a particular person, location, or activity. For example, competition rules at one gymnastics center might be different from those at another center. Can you spot the facts, opinions, and "sometimes true" facts from your interview?

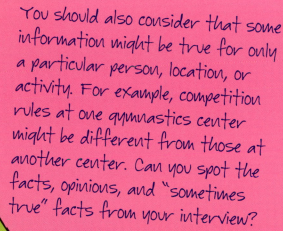

To get a copy of this activity, visit www.cherrylakepublishing.com/activities.

Last but certainly not least, send a thank-you note to your interviewee. He or she took the time to help you with this special type of research. You might even want to send a copy of your final project!

Glossary

abbreviations **(uh-breev-ee-A-shunz)** shortened forms of words

background information **(BAK-rownd in-for-MAY-shun)** research gathered before getting too involved in the project

biased **(BYE-uhst)** favoring one point of view over another

document **(DAHK-yuh-muhnt)** to make a record of something

elaborate **(i-LAB-uh-rate)** to go into more detail about something

interview **(IN-tur-vyoo)** a one-on-one or small group question-and-answer session

interviewee **(in-tur-vyoo-EE)** a person being interviewed or answering the questions

interviewers **(IN-tur-vyoo-urz)** people conducting interviews or asking the questions

quotations **(kwoh-TAY-shunz)** a word-for-word record of something someone said

summary **(SUM-uh-ree)** brief description of the main points of something that has been said or written

Find Out More

BOOKS

Marcus, Leonard S., ed. *Funny Business: Conversations with Writers of Comedy*. Somerville, MA: Candlewick Press, 2009.

Minden, Cecilia, and Kate Roth. *How to Write a News Article*. Ann Arbor, MI: Cherry Lake Publishing, 2011.

WEB SITES

Scholastic—How to Conduct an Interview

www.scholastic.com/browse/article.jsp?id=3752516

Read some helpful tips for conducting interviews.

StoryCorps—Great Questions List

http://storycorps.org/record-your-story/question-generator/list

Get some ideas of good interview questions on a variety of common topics.

Index

About the Author

Ann Truesdell is a school library media specialist and teacher in Michigan. She and her husband, Mike, love traveling and spending time with their children, James and Charlotte.